REMEMBRANCE

POEMS FOR JESUS

DEBORAH SHOSHANAH LEAL

R

REMEMBRANCE
Poems for Jesus

by Deborah Shoshanah Leal

Published by Rend Press.

ISBN: 978-1-7320077-3-4

For Jesus:
You are my First,
You are my Last.

CONTENTS

1. The Strange Divide 1
2. Rabbit 3
3. First Love 5
4. Starfish 7
5. Stardust 9
6. Planets 11
7. A Washroom Prayer 13
8. Three Threads 15
9. Gossamer 17
10. Hope 19
11. Blood 21
12. Cub 23
13. Knowing 25
14. Untelling 27
15. Jacob 29
16. Atoms 31
17. Stricken 33
18. Center of the Earth 35
19. Fear 37
20. Leaning 39
21. Inviolable 41
22. Petition 43
23. Backyard 45
24. Recovery 47
25. Veil 49
26. Adoption 51
27. Imago Dei 53
28. Dark Night 55
29. Cloudclear 57
30. Isaac 59
31. Aviva 61

32. My Heart Your Instrument 63
33. Robins Egg 65

The Strange Divide

Last night,
  I dreamed that He called out to me,

and I was startled by
  how quickly I responded

and

how far my voice carried
  beyond the
  Strange Divide.

R*abbit*

Scared little rabbit,
    backed up against
    imaginary earthworks—

there are Hands to hold you.

First Love

Give peace
    to this racing heart,
    divided long ago.

I plead remembrance
    for things forgotten,
    and blindness
    for things I should not have seen.

Keep me far from myself
    and give me something to share,
    for if I have not love,
    I am nothing.

All I had
    only ever came from You,
    so to You I return.

S*tarfish*

So I ask Him,

"How to grow back
    these broken limbs?"

Else I am starfish:
    drifting limp,
    close and seamless,
    along the silent ocean floor.

S*tardust*

Startled awake suddenly
from this Falling-Asleep,
I touched wet eyes, curiously:
(my own two,
welled up with wonder and sadness)
feeling stardust fall from them,
melting silvery.

P*lanets*

I was queen in my country,
    but You crumbled the land,
    led me out to the sand.
    Showed me a Kingdom,
    I will never understand.

Spoke softly to me,
    till I leaned on Your arms.
    So I need no more strength,
    and this is the greatest relief.

Only one Name, the one and only Name.
    This alien God with His strange planet people.
    Why He chose, no one knows.
    No one knows.
    Across space and time, no one knows.

A *Washroom Prayer*

Immerse me in Your love:
    ancient immediate
    and anchored mystical,
    droplets of everyday extravagance.

Flood me with pureness
    and simple beauty,
    for I fear I lack.

Scrub me gently down,
    rinse confusion away
    in trickling rivulets grey.
    Infuse in me, drop by drop,
    instill in me a servant's heart.

There are some things
    I simply cannot do alone.

Three Threads

Dreams push me from sleep.
I wake up to a house burnt umber,
all aslumber.
Move about the house,
this constant Thread of beauty
weaving through me.
Thread of safety wrapped around me.
Thread of passion, pulling me on.

While an evil silent
needle violent
pierces my heart, again and again.
All stabs, no stitches.

This conversation is all I ever had of you.
You cannot come in,
for you do not know of Love:
The Three Threads binding,
sewing up my life of shreds.

Once upon a time,
your absence was filled
by Threads through a needle.
Now all that I do
is stitched with those Three.

Gossamer

So much sadness.

Though my mind says mend mend mend,
    my heart just slowly bends

to weep, then send
    out floating spider-threads:

silken webs,
    to catch and touch You.

Hope

Swallowed splinters
    in my sadness,
    there's no bringing them up.

But as trembling fists tighten
    over white sheets,
    You rush in with cups
    and cups
    of bright messy hope.

I just smile
    and say
    "You've come back!"

Blood

We Pharisees,
  we laugh at what is different.
  We, all the same.
  But today, I have not come for that.
  I have come to be a child.

To dip my wond'ring hands
  in cool, crimson riches,
  slightly sticky to the touch
  and sickly to my untrained heart.

I have come to be a child,
  asking a thousand questions,
  while burying my answered head
  under a pool of calming mercury red.

I have come to be a child,
  sweeping slow arms
  in ever-widening circles,
  knowing more and more
  of a greater Love.

I have come to be a child,
  trading whimpering anger
  for a simple tub,

filled with the most extravagant Love.

You broke Your Lover's body
to leak Your Lover's blood,
and I will never understand,
yet now will never be unloved.

Cub

As You see my
little cub face
with silken ears
and matted paw,
troubled maw;
so much seen--
(can it be unseen?)
I scratch at my wounds
and growl, as fiercely
as I can muster.

So You laugh to Yourself for a moment,
then the saddest look
comes etched across Your Big Bear face,
which with all its holy sullenness
weaves the strongest invisible cords around my
weak heart.

Then reaching out a single paw
with softest fur
and strongest claw--
You beckon, with clear brown eyes.
Out You stretch,
in You draw,
near You pull me,
into the safest, warmest shadow,
where You feed me milk
and honey

and tend my crusted wounds
till they are wonderfully clean

and I am suddenly
(over a span of time)
a Little Bear--
having become not quite exactly,
but very much
like You.

Knowing

Pale paper cheek turned
    parchment,
    dry-wrinkled from tears.
    My angry will
    pitted 'gainst Yours.
    I come here often,
    I come here often.

"Everything is possible for You",
    yet this cup never passes.

Tonight,
    I am weary of knowing.
    Forever incomplete in the quest for understanding.
    So if You would,
    please take the time
    unclasp my fingers,
    bend my knee.
    Bend my will to the curve of Your own,
    so that "Not my will, but Yours be done".

Untelling

I wait for You at twilight,
    filled with pooled bits of knowing
    that are weighted down with passion
    and quieted with mourning.

Long after You've arrived (You arrived at Always),
    I cling with darkened eyes and angry mercury tears.

I know This One Here, and should not be afraid;
    but feel abandonment from generations and a mutiny of ages.

Did You feel the same in that dim garden,
    tempestuous with spirits tossed?
    Your mind brimming with untelling,
    releasing howling desire into a thin night air which burned and sparkled at Your touch;

You threw Your body on a rock,
    crying out to One You knew would close His ears to You;
    gathered such passion in Your eyes that it spilled over--
    and the wind knew it, and saw it:
    bits of blood flecking down onto Your holy, grief-hollowed hands.

amazon Gift Receipt

Send a Thank You Note

You can learn more about your gift or start a return here too.

Scan using the Amazon app or visit **https://a.co/d/aYDwRFf**

Remembrance: Poems for Jesus

Order ID: 111-2573440-3251415   Ordered on July 5, 2023

Jacob

I waited for You all night.
I would wrestle an angel
just to see Your face.
For in that holy bartering,
I could finally touch You.

Though You may wound my hip,
I saw Your ladder.
From heaven to earth,
glory exchanged over stairs
and a vision and hundreds of
wings, soft white pinions that
grazed my shoulder
and made me shiver in sacred grace.

I am awakened.
The night comes, speaks peace to all alert
and restless on their prayer beds.
The cool of the darkness
and Your well-lit way--
You are a fire in my bones,
and I am weary of holding it in.

I sent my loves and my possessions
across the dark stream
at evening,

gave them up with reckless decision.
Then I stilled my body
and quieted my soul;
waited for You in ferocity,
burning with the blessing which would soon be mine.

Atoms

The audience of earth is moving.
Every whirling atom
is craning its neck.
Matter as a whole is turning:
slightly, slowly, deliberately,
curling itself outward
to further catch the rays of His glory.
In all their lives,
they have never seen something like this.
Struck but once
with holiness,
they have been forever-after whirling:
thousands of years
in vertigo
after the murmur of His voice.

Quarks are swirling hurricanes
of nervous excitement,
agitated and joyous for the Wedding,
to hear His voice again (like the Great Before).
Space, time, and light,
all in earnest,
bend and undulate to His breaths and movements.

Look at the Created.
All the earth praises Him,
while we flip our minds
and spin ourselves in circles

and wonder why we do not feel
the delicate turns and curves
of His mighty, terrifying Will.

The atoms can smell God.
The light can smell God.
(They remember,
they taste the memory of Him.)

From the lint
to the elephants
to the dry grey hollow
in the corner of the ceiling:
every sparkling, delicate
speck of creation
is groaning for His return.

O the groaning
of Nature and Loving,
spiraled together
and soon to be reckoned with.

Stricken

Thought I saw You only in beauty.
    But in this sorrow,
    I see You.
    Even here.

A Man of sorrows,
    familiar with suffering.
    You gathered up our infirmities,
    though it cut You, body to soul.
    You know what it is to be stricken,
    to be silent and unheld.

For I have never loved You more
    than in this moment,
    at my most shipwrecked
    and fragile,
    between the wind and the thin leaf trembling--
    I am only this slice of air, this slivered fear;
    while You are everything beyond.

Center of the Earth

I have never been to this place before.
    I am pulled into the underground.

Journey to the center of the earth,
    to the center of Yourself.

I am struck by the quantity of light
    found in such an intimate place.

Dim glimmering of crystal light;
    such a delicate place.

F*ear*

I want to only fear Your Ghost,
    but found
    I'm fast afraid of fear itself.

I've clutched it first to fill,
    failed to bend it to Your will.

How long, oh Lord.
    How long?

Leaning

In the dark night,
    tempestuous with spirits tossed,
    it is not my mind that tells.
    Tonight, to You, I whispered:
    "My heart knows You,
    my heart knows You"
    and some Spirit leapt within.

It has always known You.
    Before I spoke a Name,
    I spoke in groanings ever deepened--
    deep calling to deep.
    So You washed over me,
    till You broke me into beauty,
    till I learned to come up leaning.

Inviolable

His blood speaks of worth.
    His blood is leaden and pungent,
    mixed with incense
    and flecks of myrrh.

Heavy red mercury,
    spilling, swirling down the artery.
    Trickling down a trail,
    like acid down the Veil.

Magic soaks His spine.
    Tingling indigo bruise--
    standing to the side,
    waiting.

Sweet iron-smelling blood,
    thorns raking head of dingy, sweaty curls.
    Dark eyes dim,
    sparkling sweet with defiant undefeat.

Drum snaps:
    undead! undread!
    Bass pushes forth,
    rips and blooms in music.
    That incessant blood, unbending,

slippery unkillable medicine;
sonorous trembling music,
flute-soft blood breaking metal diamond scorn.

Petition

Untremble this heart,
    strengthen these knees.
    Forgive the sins in which I tarry,
    forgive my oft-repeated pleas.

Untangle mingled motives dark.
    Fan feeble flame which once was spark.
    Snatch me fast afar from sin,
    too long tended, nursed within.

Unfurrow this brow, knitted in fright.
    Teach how to pace the paths of light.
    Never take Thy hand from me,
    for I am naught, if not with Thee.

Backyard

The trees in the backyard looked like Eden.

The old wooden fence shone bright white-grey from harsh sunlight,
    while I knelt in the cool of shade,
    porch lit low with cold pebble comfort.
    I sat still, ears wide open:
    chirp of a few lone birds
    telegraphing secret words,
    one dry brown leaf scuttling by.

Every smooth blade of grass
    is miraculous in its place,
    the coo of bird and sigh of leaves up high,
    moving slight and soft–
    the grey rough bark calls out to me,
    "Come! Come! Come and climb, dear one, little one;
    climb like you did in your youth."

And I am overwhelmed,
    intoxicated by the smell of damp earth and verdant grass and the loam of the land.

How could I ever tear myself away?
    I want to run back to it all,
    to my soft childhood bower:

moss where I was cradled and nurtured
and fascinated daily;
ten whole minutes staring at one
little wild ant–that changed my whole world,
it altered the course of my life.

And so He meant it to be.
Didn't You?
Yes, I see it now. Papa, You made me this way,
and fashioned the earth with a smile on Your face,

so that as a child, when the afternoon sunlight slanted low,
before the milky moonlight rinsed the earth in pearly sweetness,
I would slide open the porch door,
heart rushing fast,
and smile at all this Glory,
because You loved me, and that is why

the trees in the backyard looked like Eden.

R*ecovery*

Perhaps I have not noticed my God.
    So I speak:
    Have me, all.
    Slip this softly from these hands.

I long to lengthen upward,
    to stretch and stand and tread Your Way,
    illumined with faith, perfervid with joy,
    Your strange wilderness Light pulling me on.

Veil

It is in the stillness that I see You
    when the swirls of life
    billow gently to the side
    and You come close.

You come in close,
    and from far away I can see You coming

up from the wilderness,
    up to my wilderness,
    to the cave where I nestle
    upon the pillow,
    upon the rock of You.

I have built You an altar in my heart,
    You have built Yourself a temple of my body.
    The two are knit and intertangled;
    I cannot separate what You have put together.

The only thing You rend
    is separation;
    You split a veil to put a bridal veil of glory o'er my face

Oh, the closeness of You,
    the reaching out and touching Your cheek,

the memorizing of Your face,
the daily watching of Your eyes.

You see me,
and I live for the moment
that I see You,
(it shimmers and)
it shivers
from my skin
to my spirit deep within.

Adoption

Knit within my belly
    the rooting and grounding of Your love,
    the umbilical cord,
    You to me:
    the Adoption.

This cord You knit
    tethers me to You.
    Woven by Your flesh,
    (once black and blue),
    and filled with all manner of richness,
    this good and perfect gift,
    rich red from Blood shed,
    from the Father of lights, not changing like shifting shadows,
    no, there is no turning in This Love.

With a mighty hand and outstretched arm
    You gathered me to Yourself,
    all Your compassions kindled;
    Your heart turned over within itself,
    and scooped me up from the fall.

Abba, Abba, Your love is so full;
    my soul never knew till now.

Imago Dei

"Made in the image of God,"
that's what You told me.
For so long I thought life was a chore,
aching upon the rising and upon the lying down,
my body something to be fought or tamed,
not a wonder of life.
(It was always: too little, too much.)

But that night
just before the dusky dawn rising,
You poured crumbs of butter-yellow hope-light
down into my hungry heart

and I was shining.

No more dark-grey cobwebs
twisted 'round my eyes,
musty thin veil of soft light-grey dust,
hanging 'round my head as a weighted metal shell,
sobbing silent behind dust and dread.

In my heart, so sudden, rose a song,

and as I trace my fingers 'round the
edge of this glorious skin,

I smile, so still,
take the deepest breaths,
and I sing.
Ringing out of my heart, and O, Your
hope, I could taste it! sweet as balm,
sweet as honey to the lips of my untrained heart.

Dark Night

When the night
    folds its dark blue fingers
    like ribbons weaving smoothly above me,
    my breathing slows and calms
    and I am covered in deepest peace
    and sleep.

When the dark night,
    dream night,
    folds its fingers over me,
    I feel You knitting me
    (me, one formerly in pieces):
    You circle Hands around my ribs
    and gently draw me close,
    softly pull me in.
    (It is only here that I feel free enough to breathe.)

There is no touch like Yours.
    Your shouts are whispers,
    Your fierceness sweet.
    There is a Lion within the Lamb:
    yes, it was the Soft Voice that startled me.

From One Wounded to another,
    enfold gently, You sing songs in the night:
    "Only Me, child. Think only on Me,

and I promise you a world you could never dream".

For in the weaving I am waiting;
when this dizzy heart is breaking,
it's Your face I reach out and touch.

Cloudclear

Here upon this mountain,
all is muffled silent.
Your cloud of glory
blurs out all I see.
Your cloud of glory,
thick and heavy,
holds me still, sets me free.

And the brightness of Your countenance
settles on my skin,
for radiance such as this
cannot be restrained.

Imprint on me Your heart-glowing:
more than matches,
more than the dry dust that moves about the earth,
so eager to be set ablaze—

And as a man talks with a friend,
in this way my thirsting eyes will be rewarded:
shining lashes wet with clarity.

I*saac*

Your face is a symphony.
    Looking down from above, I see:

the curl of your lashes,
    the smooth of your skin,
    nose like daddy,
    smile like mommy.

You are a whole wide world of miracles,
    of cells and synapses,
    a whole wild earth turning perfect
    on its axis.

Your eyes are like stars.
    I cradle galaxies
    between my arms;
    your eyes are like stars.

Aviva

Shadow-dust glistens, diamond-dust listens.
Fades together, then apart,
shimmering 'round a cool-flicker halo.
Midnight-dust begets black and white grains,
penumbra hovers and glows.
Your lashes: two butterfly wings, pressed up against my own.
Face to face with the face within my womb.

I saw you in dreams.
The sweet smell of your dark silken hair, nestled into my shoulder.
You shivered, and only I could comfort you.

I'll smile in the moonlight,
hold you till you sleep.
Small hands softly unfolded,
breaths slow in gentle peace.

My Heart Your Instrument

Here in the night,
in the shaded grey shadows,
in the gentle and perseverant pains
that prod me from sleep—
my heart is awake to You.

I have nothing else,
my body empty.
My heart is awake to You.

What is within?
What is this? intangible air as a Finger,
laying Itself upon the string of my heart,
strings stretched almost to breaking?
No noise, silent,
no words, vacant.
Hollow, You've hallowed me holy.

Here in the night,
a hum, invisible,
a sound, intangible.
Drawing notes from me, yet never from me.
I bend to Your Bow, hold myself steady,
You sweep above me, You've made Yourself ready.
You've remade me hale and healed,
though silent, laden-heavy.

Your music will surround me,
and out of emptiness will arise
holiness, wholeness,
the swirling of Your melody.

R*obins Egg*

I hold Your eggshell promise in my hand.
    Peppered, flecked, and mottling,
    cool and heavy,
    thin as paper,
    holding multitudes inside.

Made in the USA
Middletown, DE
06 July 2023

34611440R00045